PETS WE LOVE

RABBIT

TURTLE

GOLDFISH

CAT

DOG

HAMSTER

PARTS OF OUR BODY

EYES

ARMS

MOUTH

NOSE

FINGERS

HEAD

THINGS WE DO IN THE CLASSROOM

READ

CLOSE THE BOOK

DRAW

COLOR

OPEN THE BOOK

RAISE THE HAND

THINGS WE USE AT SCHOOL

NOTEBOOK

PENCIL SHARPENER

SCHOOLBAG

RULER

PEN

PENCIL CASE

MY WONDERFUL TOYS

SKATE

DOLLHOUSE

BIKE

ROBOT

TEDDY BEAR

BALL

Macmillan do Brasil
Rua José Félix de Oliveira 383
Granja Viana – 06708-645 – Cotia, SP, Brasil
Atendimento ao Professor: São Paulo – Capital (0XX11) 4613 2278
Demais localidades: 0800 168877
Fax: (0XX11) 4612 6098
E-mail: elt@macmillan.com.br
Visite nosso website: www.macmillan.com.br

INTERNAL CODE
978-66-7418-162-7
9786674181627